Convergence: A Neighborhood

Convergence: A Neighborhood

Poems by

Harry Moore

Cover design by Shay Culligan
Cover image by Harry Moore
Author photo by Harry Moore

ISBN: 979-8-90146-814-2

Kelsay Books
502 South 1040 East, A-119
American Fork, Utah 84003
Kelsaybooks.com

Acknowledgments

My thanks to the following venues where poems in this collection previously appeared or are forthcoming:

Alabama State Poetry Society (Spring 2025 Contest): "Hunter's Remorse" (1st place)

Pensive: A Global Journal of Spirituality and the Arts: "What the Sages Say"

The Penwood Review: "Sign"

Plainsongs: "The Percipient," "The Stationary Bike"

Poets' Choice: "Fashion Statement," "In Medias Res"

Slipstream: "The Thin-Spun Life"

Trajectory: "Long Division," "Elegy," "My Friend Is Dead"

Underwood: "Venus"

Word histories are taken from *Webster's New World College Dictionary,* 4th ed.

Contents

Where the Twain Meet

Named for a Northern city and an English
duke, oak-shaded Albany began as

New Town over a century ago, settled
by Yankees working the L & N. Old Town

lingers a mile away, its aged bank riddled
with musket balls, houses burned by

Union troops, all its churches named First,
its restaurant honoring a steamboat captain.

Our restaurant is a bistro, and Delano Park,
designed by a man from Chicago, is named

for the New Deal President. The Anglican
church was built with funds from the City

of Brotherly Love. On our street signs,
block by block, names of warring generals

alternate—Johnston, Grant, Jackson, Sherman.
My Arizona neighbors build a rock garden,

drive their daughter to Ithaca, where she
studies political science. Election signs

are mixed, here progressive, there retro—
still not sure the war is over.

What Do You Do?

< Fr *retirer: re-*, back + *tirer,* to draw

Now that he's retired, *drawn back*
from classroom lectures saying what
Milton meant; from marking essays,

freshmen flinging phrases at some
unseen target; from tired committees
making up their mission, he wakes to

gratitude for breath, morning's first light,
coffee, berries, wrens, poems, all the ways
words can move across a page, every

day an orchard ripe for picking.
He walks, friends drop in unannounced,
cousins e-mail, dried tethers grow supple

with use. He marvels at maples, the massive
girth of willow oaks. Barking dogs come
to kennel, theology is a treasure hunt,

science a county fair. Time lies about him
like a lake, an air he breathes, no longer
spent, wasted, saved, or killed. At evening,

Venus hangs above the steeple to the west,
bulbous, bright, unmoving in the night sky.

Fashion Statement

The truth must dazzle gradually . . .
—Emily Dickinson

He is a minimalist, he says,
hardly moving when he dances,
preferring blue and gray to red,
hanging three wreaths out front
for a Historic District Christmas.
He drives a silver microvan.

Does he fear exuberance
because the gods might grudge
a festive air—hoarding a private
peace beyond their gaze? Or

does he lack the confidence
of a brilliant scarf or tie, fearing
the wrong note, embarrassment
the worst fate of all?

Or does he keep an inner fire, doling
warmth in pleasantries and spare phrases
while jungle drums pulse his veins
in wild dance?

On the Limits of Rationalism

Our sturdy bulldog gathers expectation
like a balloon taking on air as he waits
for his morning walk. On the leash, he

rushes past neighbors' houses, past
the Presbyterian church, the fenced yard
where Mack the collie has moved away,

to the park, where we loop the mile trail.
Despite all quieting words, he pushes
ahead like a harness racer pacing for

the finish line. Leaning into the collar
as he sees the slight lady and black Lab
ahead, he constricts his own breath, chest

heaving as he closes in. Back home, spent,
having reduced his walk time by five per cent,
he flops down panting inside the gate.

The Reluctant Walker

Our spayed rescue hound tugs against
the leash, sniffing the base of oak, pecan,
power-line poles, fire hydrants, plunging
her nose deep into piss-bitten monkey grass,
inhaling the past, ignoring half-tame squirrels
that dig in lawns or flirt their tails from stolid
hackberry trunks.
                                        Then she stands erect, still,
eyes far away in some lost wood where she
bays up a tall poplar hiding a lithe raccoon,
or where she runs with muscular males—
Blue Ticks, Redbones, Julys, Walkers—
in untiring strides after fox and deer that
lure them on through forests where leaves
fall forever.
                                  Back home, she rushes to a
pan of two measured cups of Healthy Weight
dry food laced with real turkey.

Hunter's Remorse

House sparrows clamor in a neighbor's eaves
and from maple and crepe myrtle timid wrens
hurl their lusty cries across city blocks:
PEET-suh, PEET-suh, PEET-suh, PEET-suh.
Redbirds whistle, blue jays complain shrilly,
flickers drum metal chimney tops, and robins
querk querk querk their mild alarm at walkers
and their dogs.

                                        When he was ten, he stalked
grass birds in pasture pines, thrashers in thorny
plum bush thickets, knocking a blue jay from
a tall loblolly, along dead-eye aim glimpsing
the bb's copper arc before the telling thud.
To quell a rising conscience, he fed spoils
to the cat that followed him, weeping once
over a wren he mistook for a sparrow.

Walking Daisy:
Prayer on Gordon Drive

I am moved by fancies that are curled
Around these images, and cling:
The notion of some infinitely gentle
Infinitely suffering thing.
—T. S. Eliot. "Preludes"

The Temples in the Victorian cottage
have a baby girl. They push her carriage
along the sidewalk, towing the Lab
and Weimaraner. The Lab, now gray
about the muzzle, walks stiffly and
lags behind.

White-haired Mr. Wallace shuffling
on the porch of the blond brick
behind a walker has died, and
Mrs. Wallace no longer sits coaxing
our hound into tail-wagging yowls
of greeting. Near a sign saying
the empty house is for sale, the dog
looks toward the porch and whines.

The brick rancher on the corner where
the pasteboard sign said, "Don't let your dog
crap on my grass," is vacant, the large lady
with the barking Pekingese in the back yard
absent. Everything went at auction.
Today, workers peel shingles from the roof,
and a woman and small boy move boxes
from a black pickup into the house.

From courts across the street, I hear
the regular *thunk . . . thunk . . . thunk*
of tennis balls. Tony, happy West Coast
retiree in lime green and spandex,
jogs the park trail beside festooning
crepe myrtles. In tight pants and top,
dark-haired Mrs. Clancy stretches while
her twin boys play about the stroller.

At the brown frame two-story where conical
hydrangea blooms hang at the carport corner,
Mrs. Poole's husband has moved to a
nursing home, and her fat Lab has disappeared.
"I had to send Lady to heaven," she says,
picking up her paper; "she had cancer."

In the neat Tudor, Pearl lives alone. Jim
died years ago of mesothelioma. He worked
in an asbestos factory during college one summer.
She gives my granddaughter a book about wolves.

My friend in the ivied brick is recovering well,
she says. Her daughters are blossoming
and she has peace. Beside the pen where
a German shepherd barks and rattles the gate,
Rose of Sharon blooms day after day
through hottest June.

Perchance to Dream

The old farm lies rooted beneath
trim historic streets, crab grass

we fought in cotton fields breaking
out beside the neighbor's new

wrought iron fence—with pokeweed,
sawbriers, cow-itch vines, and three

unmistakable stalks of poison oak.
Squirrels flee across leaf-cluttered

yards, and Rose of Sharon blooms
beside a Tudor brick on Sherman.

From Westminster peale chimes
of "Softly and Tenderly": "ye who

are weary, come home." Oak roots
strain, crack hundred-year sidewalks,

surging up from depths of dark soil,
forms rising from a restless sleep.

Trouble in Eden

When the wisteria vine large
as my arm snaked around
the crepe myrtle trunk out back—
like a serpent strangling Laocoön—
infesting the tree's foliage with
purple clusters and beanlike pods,

I sawed the thick vine in two
at its base, releasing its grip,
watching petals fall for days
and, over the winter, picking up
brittle sticks and dead vine fragments
that fell from the tree.
This hot June,
the liberated crepe myrtle blossoms
pink all around,
like a large satellite dish,
its top lopped away by city workers
making space for wires strung along
the alley.
Meanwhile, wisteria shoots
from the truncated base lick upward,
looking for purchase.

Mark But This:
The Author Falls Ill of a Fever

Kept in, laid up, burning, burning,
he stumbles against bed posts,
sloshes coffee on kitchen tiles,
soup on place mats. His fever,

brushing 104, hangs doggedly
at 102.5. An upside, he notes, is
crisp internal clarity as he wanders
from table to bath to bed, drifting

in and out of sleep, the lush images
surprising him, shadows on a cliff wall
coalescing into sinister eyes, nose,
an entire face. One scene makes

him weep, his mother and brother
standing on a street, talking, beyond
his reach. Mostly he flits, joining
Mariska Hargitay chasing perps,

trading glances over drinks as he
reads nuances of her mouth and eyes.
Then, after bed-drenching sweat washes
him back to normal, the doctor calls:

his incendiary assailant rode inside
a blood-sucking tick, furtive, crawling,
tiny, one he might have crushed against
his thumbnail. The meds will hunt

the culprit down. Now—staggering
to the john in half darkness—he
wonders if these inner fires raised
only bravado, swollen confidence

on all questions of diet or pills his
exhausted wife seemed not to understand.
Or did the mind rise above Earth's
cold and sluggish air, dance in primal

firelight to drumbeats in the blood,
leap with agility and grace from one
dreamy scene to another, as staunch
defenders drove the invader out?

The Stationary Bike

Sleek and spare, it tells on glowing
dials how long, how far, how many
calories burned. Four bars of tension
for the pulse, then six, then a wild
ten as the heart settles, finds its pace.

Nothing much moves as I pedal
weightless on worn knees, pumping
past a granddaughter's 29th birthday,
past my father's birth a century ago,
through Thanksgiving, 40 years of
marriage, months of pandemic fading
in the rear-view mirror I do not have.

Zooming through poetry readings,
workshops, contests, a class on the
neglected Apocrypha, board meetings
that creep into one's solitude,
                                        masking
for groceries, wine, gin, beer, brandy,
a daring foray into outdoor dining
before winter settles in,
                                long distance calls,
cross-continent Facetime with grandkids
doing cartwheels, headstands as we chat,
unbelievably tall across months we have
not touched.

Sweatshirt damp, heart
surging—ten miles, 240 calories, the slim
slice of pecan pie I topped off lunch with—
I dismount, get shaky legs under me,
head toward a shower, email, Chinese
take-out for dinner, decisions about
Masterpiece, The Office, Death in
Paradise during another evening,

toward Facebook condolences for a
friend, news about crowded hospitals,
spiking numbers, old people growing
lonely in nursing homes, a vaccine
like a pace rabbit we pedal toward,
furiously, in place.

Lying Low

> *home* < IE base **kei-,* to lie,
> homestead: basic sense "place
> where one lies; dwelling"

Earth spins, stars peer through the dark
as I stoop for the morning paper. Tall
oaks add to their girth, circle by circle,
roots lifting, cracking the sidewalk.

Oceans simmer, winds hurl north from
a Gulf hurricane, rains beat, drench, seep
between concrete roof tiles.
                                        The virus clings
like beggar lice to the woven fabric
of our lives, rides the air like smoke
from a surging wildfire.
                                        Protestors march,
smash windows; police chase, barricade,
choke, shoot.
                    My friends cocoon themselves
in likes and outrage.
                                        I rise at five, sip coffee,
munch berries, trail mix, scribble, talk phone
to phone with a daughter and granddaughter,
ride the unmoving bike, venture into a vacant
park.

My wife walks the house, counts steps,
circles the sofa and table where an orchid leans
toward light, veers into the dining room and
repeats the loop.
Home is where we lie,
pull back, duck, dig in, stay put, waiting for
some voice to say all's clear, we are safe, we
can come out.

Pandemic Song

> *grace, gratitude,* and *bard:*
> from IE base **gwer-,*
> to lift up the voice, praise

In the backyard garden, redbirds
cheep, sparrows bustle, chitter,
jays scream *DIE! DIE!* From
a cherry laurel's dense foliage an
Eastern towhee sounds its Southern
jo-REE, jo-REE. Doves coo and mourn
from tall wires beside the alley,
and a hidden wren sings, *Miss you!*
Miss you!
                All voice is song, surging
upstream toward the spawning pool—
hymns, ditties, oracles, orations, cantatas—
beside tall zinnias lingering through
late summer, hummingbirds buzzing
from feeder to flower, a place of
beauty too deep and fecund to sort.

There's pain enough, for sure, storms,
fires, a rampant virus, hunger we toss
money towards, beatings, shootings,
tribal wars with words, the clock
winding down on everything.

But
farther back, beneath, in, around all
these, an unbidden urge to *praise,*
give thanks, to hear in the *bard's*
lofty cadence, in every child's shout
and laughter, a *grace* we cannot lose.

Of this—with cicadas drilling deep
into the silence, with crickets whose
fiddling jig is their music—we sing,
join the motley chorus.

Long Division

Low walls I once cleared
in a single leap, I now climb
stone by stone,
                    routes that
sprang to mind across an
entire city, I now parse
street by street,
                    names that
came quick and whole, now
emerge willy nilly, one
consonant at a time, and still
lie mangled.
                    Age that was
once a number, now divides
to decades, scores, three-fourths
of a century.
                              Spring
after spring our hundred-year
magnolia—four giant columns
towering toward heaven—
showers leaves across the roof,

and I climb a tall ladder, one
rung after another, to clean
clogged gutters my wife says

I should leave to other hands,
other heads half my age.

A Sign

On the steep roof
of the laundry room, a dove
pecks at a tangle of dead
jasmine vines, darting in and
striking repeatedly, like
a snake-killing dog unafraid
of fangs. Eyeing me, she
backs away, then returns
to seize and shake stiff twigs.

Is it peace she is after, jasmine
a stand-in where olives do not grow?
Has she survived centuries of bloody war,
pillage, feuding, rape, ready now
to bear her branch to some
stranded ark-builder seeking
a new world?

Or is she merely determined
and dense, coming back
time after time seeking sticks
for the nest on a narrow ledge
out front, where sharp-eyed cats
wait for any fledgling to fall?

The Thin-Spun Life

It was the rarest of unlikely accidents.
—City Utilities General Manager

How many wheels, through the years
and decades, whirred and bumped across
the eight-inch, ten-pound cast iron cap

flush with the surface of Highway 20
just beyond the railroad overpass?
How much asphalt around the water-

valve box eroded and crumbled before
the cap sat just off kilter? At what speed
and angle at 4:07 p.m. on a Friday in April

did the white sedan's right front tire strike
the edge of the heavy lid so that it rose
wobbling like a bad punt, cleared the red

pickup, and smashed through the windshield
of the dark Corolla just behind? At what
velocity did the metal disk strike the forehead

of the woman driving home from work
with gardening on her mind—shutting off
the light, the heart's steady pump, all

awareness of other cars, puffy clouds
beyond the river, of her husband at home,
two daughters, four grandchildren, all

the memories of her three score years?
Who did not notice the cracks, decay,
the iron lid leaning awry? What draftsman

drew these wild converging vectors?

In Medias Res

< L, *into the midst of things*

The epic begins after
war breaks out, Achilles
sulking in his tent, Grendel
devouring drunken thanes,
Satan's cohorts dazed
on the burning lake—
the backstory edging in
after the fact.
We all start
in the middle of someone's
story, the brother five years in,
older father who has quit his
whiskey, mother young and
hopeful. Somebody is President,
an uncle away at war, the market
up or down. Nobody gets
a fresh start.
Or a curtain drop
at the end. We leave the play
in progress, the plot massive
and multiple—incremental
emergence of *homo sapiens,*
the slow warming of Earth,
tilted whirl of galaxies, two nations
raining rockets on each other,

some idle word or gross insult
left hanging, the plan to sod
the yard undone,
as we yearn
for a tidying word, some
small victory, *dènoument,*
before we fail to wake in bed
one morning or sink beside
the park trail while sparrows
chitter in the undergrowth.

Elegy

althea < Gr *althaia,* lit., healer,
wild mallows, formerly used medicinally

Across miles and through months of silence
words connected us, a note saying she
liked the poems, a link to a *Times* piece on
Stephen Dunn or John Prine, a book dropped
by the door on Meister Eckhart—or a novel on
how trees talk and may save us—something
she had read and thought I might like. News
from Nashville, the job with preschoolers,
a course at Vanderbilt, the cozy chapel there,
bike rides with Laurie, the long trek to
Santiago, guarded candor about her struggles,
the joke that "friends in rehab" put her
in one of my poems.

Now the silence
is a knife, as our old street bursts into spring,
white pears, cherries, dogwoods, the gnarled
redbud by the Deasons', rich pink petals
erupting from the bark, daffodils, forsythia
limbs draped like willow, trailing gold like
a fountain.

The brick gable
on her old house, sharp as a steeple, is
stripped of ivy, the yard wild and ragged
with white clover, dandelion, chickweed,
fleabane, and crawling vetch. The new
residents are phantoms out of sight.

Weeks from now, when her namesake
Rose of Sharon blooms pink and white
by the alley on Eighth, I will think of her,
but *althea* will not, as it promises, heal.
It will say she left too suddenly, too soon.

The mailbox remains empty, the stoop
by the front door bare. From a budding
oak beside the street, a redbird flings its
piercing note into the April air.

My Friend Is Dead

In the re-purposed Turner Memorial
Baptist Church at the Iron Hand Brewery
named for a city father with a hard

prosthesis I plow through a flight of blonde
and amber ale, chocolate stout, and Extra
Special Bitter as my wife and I wait

to split a whole-plate cheese and chicken
quesadilla and two sides of coleslaw.
The Bitter evokes a British pub, with

tongue and groove pine walls, pine
tables, cut-down pine church pews, and
a curving pine bar floating securely

over the former baptistery where
candidates rose to new life.
                                        My friend

who loved Manhattans is dead, and we
must rise at 4:00 a.m. tomorrow and drive
the length of a state to honor him—to read

to a gathering of mourners about some world
with no pain, no tears, no disease, et cetera—
no trembling hand arrested in mid-reach

awaiting a neuron spark to complete
the gesture, no foot suspended mid-step,
no words straining through a thin whisper,

no eyes reflecting the trapped mind that
remembers too much.
                                                  Better to be missed

than remembered, he liked to say, and we
will weep at this new and ragged absence,
a restaurant chair where he does not sit,

the dull silence as we stare at the menu,
strained laughter over ice cream for dessert.
Exiting the pub beneath a British Railways

sign through the church's former narthex,
we walk up State Street toward Joachim
and Dauphin, to the A & M Peanut Store

where my wife bought cashews and bridge
mix as a child, to Three Georges Candy with
a praline recipe old as World War I, and

our last stop, the Haunted Book Shop, in
its smart new location—knowing he would
have loved the brew pub church, raising

a glass of blonde or amber, Bitter or stout.

The Percipient

after Hardy

My friends speak of the dead
as if they were on vacation
or shopping in the city and
will be home before dark.

Not as if they have gone
where they were before they came
and now ride the orbiting earth,
lurk among the stars, and

mingle with iris and pansies
in the backyard bed, with
robins and redbirds breaking
the pre-dawn silence,

neighbors' dogs yapping
after alley walkers, greening
buds of crepe myrtle creeping
toward purple bloom. As if

they aren't always with us.

Terra Firma

I wake in quiet dark at 5:00 a.m.
my wife of 40 years warm beside me.
A tall waning moon brightens
the window. The ceiling fan
creaks a steady beat. Outside
an a.c. unit hums. Sparrows,
redbirds, wrens are silent.

> Earth-bound, we walk
> a gritty soil above a molten core,
> seething cauldron, surging up,
> pressing out, shaking the world,
> bursting mountaintops, bathing
> slopes, towns in steaming lava.

Breathing deep, I give thanks
for air, life, food, comfort, for all
of eighty years. I pray for peace,
safety, healing for the beautiful child
with melanoma, for a friend after
throat surgery, spots of joy for all of us.

> We cling to a spinning orb
> like a top, whirling faster than
> sound, leaving all talk behind.

I rise, move among shadows
toward the familiar kitchen, news
of the city council, yesterday's

Yankees score, two cups of dark
Sumatra brew, complex and earthy,
Fair Trade Certified, and a slice
of left-over quiche.

Racing through space, we loop
a middling star too hot to touch,
a million miles each waking day,
seventy in a breath, a score
for every spasm of the heart.

Soon, I'll sort whites, colored,
delicates, towels, four loads
in the new Maytag on yet
another day.

We float in a cluster of *galactic*
stars, like *milk* sprayed across
the night sky, our spiral neighbors
like ballroom dancers gliding,
circling, twirling, in ever
widening moves.

Venus

Bright in the pre-dawn sky, just
to the right of the Geddes's tall oak
as I bend for the morning paper—
and in the evening hanging over

the wide street to the west—it
is not a stalled plane, meteorite,
pulsing star, or sun with its own
spinning system, but a reflector,

mirror in the neighborhood, a planet
out for its own fling. It's not that
I want to go there or that if I did
I would go out in fiery glory

or find its miasmic clouds a cover
for the day's work. It isn't even
always there, playing hide-and-seek
with the tilting earth, now left,

right, low, high, dim, or starkly bright
as circling seasons come and go.
Its beam is hope, surviving the dark
west to appear before dawn

just to the right of the Geddes's
tall oak, a promise of light, springtime,
summer's heat, harvest, faithful return
in an uncertain world.

Trees

You have to lay your hand
                    on the cool bark
rough sturdy oak, barnacled hackberry,
papery river birch, late summer
                    crape myrtle
smooth as a newborn's skin.

You have to look
                    at the leaves
their shapes, veins, edges, sweetgum
like stars, gingko a medley of tiny fans,
serrated elm, post oak like puzzle parts,
sleek, shiny tupelo,
                    how water oak
widens toward the tip.

You have to feel
                    the roots
beneath your feet, spreading wide
digging deep, drawing water, iron,
zinc, phosphorus, potassium, up
a thin membrane beneath the bark
along every limb
                    to the smallest
outermost twig.

You have to name
hickory, poplar,
serviceberry, cedar, blackgum, sycamore,
swamp white oak, hornbeam, holly,
pine, redbud,
brittle bradford pear.

You have to see
in each tree's trunk
something stalwart in ourselves, through
wind, rain, storm, drought, thrusting up
against time's drag, reaching out into sky,
anchored in earth
where once a seed fell.

Who Is Wise Among You?

< IE base **w(e)di,* to see, know
> L *videre,* to see

To be *wise* is to *see* clearly, to have
vision, without which we perish.

See what, though? What *is?* Gravel
crunching beneath my sneakers
on the park trail? A stark water oak
congested with mistletoe? The rescue
hound, head on paws, breathing her last?
Is it to take in earth and sky, ride
time's drift, its torrent, the slow spiral?

Is it to *name* what we see? Sweet blooming
abelia, healing althea, speckled aucuba,
purple spiderwort and creamy Lenten roses
along the alley? Is it to remember *single-tree*
and *trace chains* by which Ada pulled
the plow in my father's field?
Is it to *connect*
intricate strands of the web that holds us—
freeze the pattern in a moment's flash,
how a pulsing heart catches an ocean's
tide beneath the moon, an electron
mirrors Earth's orbit, a falling leaf
every death?

Or do the wise see *through*
all spectacle, peel it away like a garment,
touch and pierce the world's body, take in
its breath, resting finally in the quiet dark,
deeper than all seeing, where in fallow soil
the seed awaits its season?

What the Sages Say

1

amœba < Gr *amoibē,* change

This, said the bearded scientist
in his lab, is how it works.

Shape-shifting, uncontained,
the *amœba* surrounds its prey—

dead or alive. Hunter, gatherer,
scavenger, it hugs, absorbs, then

splits, doubling down. Giving no
ground, it survives, a moving maw,

all-consuming self.

2

seed < IE base *sē(i)-,* to cast, let fall

That, said the bearded hermit from
his cave, is hardly half; the soil

is richer than we know. Bound into
its form, the *seed*—acorn, maple,

wheat—lets go, falls to ground.
Dying, giving up its single self, it

bursts new life, surges to the light,
yielding stalk, branches, leaves, fruit,

rich harvest, a field of ripened grain.

One

We who are many crave
to be one, from the moment
the expelled and wandering egg
collides with wiggling sperm,

like long lost friends meeting
over dinner or lovers wrapped
in desperate embrace. We are
pushed, pulled, ripped from

the warm confined womb,
spend our days severing cell
by cell the primal connection,
seeking in shared food, drink,

parties, feasts, banquets, orgies
the union we once had.
                                        Jagged
like shards from a shattered urn,

we yearn to lose ourselves, meld
into water we swim in, into the
park landscape brilliant with gold
and red maples in fall, lucid

stars on a cold night, a room
warm with chatter and laughter
among friends and family,
                                        finding
there, in clamor or in quiet,
a music we once slept to.

Convergence: Where All Roads Meet

A century in, the park is a mosaic:
black families flying birthday balloons
under pavilions,
                                        Hispanic children racing
over the grass after soccer balls,
                                                                        inmates
from a group home clustering together,
chatting, looking at phones,
                                                                old men
walking shih tzus, yorkies, chihuahuas,
around the one-mile trail,
                                                        young men
with Labs, heelers, muzzled bulldogs,
thc woman with two corgis cutting
a corner to spare me their eager greeting,
a youth biking past, wishing good morning,

two green-backed June bugs belly-up on the trail,
none swarming above the grass this year.

My childhood farm erupting beside the path—
yellow-blooming bitterweed that invaded
the pasture and spiked our milk, now hugging
hard-beaten soil, ducking the mower blade,
a sprig of coffee weed, American sickleweed,
tall along the trail to the barn when I was five.

White, black, Hispanic city workers zipping
on lawn tractors across the long grassy slope,
others wielding whizzing weed trimmers
around trees, benches, poles.

On asphalt
basketball courts with shiny orange goals
and new nets, young men scraping, scuffing,
clamoring in spirited pick-up games.
At park
center a red-tail hawk spreading wings, landing
at its nest atop a tall loblolly pine.
Behind
white-blooming hydrangea, river birches,
and the tall dragonfly sculpture, children
laughing, shouting on slides and swings,
surfaces padded, gently sloped, gates open
to all.
Hard by, shrieking girls and boys running
in and out of jetting streams on the splash pad.

A transparent deity lives here, in the hundred-year
willow oak beside Eighth, in the intricate twining
of people as they come and go, in the shrill cry
of a blue jay, the gritty soil of the path gripped
by stiff-bladed goose grass and crisscrossed
by rows of busy ants.

All races, ages,
men, women, toddlers, babies in strollers,
dogs, birds, trees, years past, present, dirt, sky,
loungers, refugees, wanderers, serious walkers,
runners—from city, suburbs, farms long gone
fallow.
Here, strangeness falls away and
everything belongs—the garden where we
all began and can't stop coming back to.

Notes

"Fashion Statement." Epigraph is from Emily Dickinson's poem beginning, "Tell all the Truth but tell it slant."

"Perchance to Dream." Title is from Hamlet's "To be or not to be" soliloquy: "To die, to sleep; / To sleep, perchance to dream—ay, there's the rub" (3.1.64–65).

"Mark But This." Title is from the opening of John Donne's seduction poem "The Flea": "Mark but this flea, and mark in this, / How little that which thou deniest me is."

"A Sign." See Genesis 8:10–12 (KJV): "And again he [Noah] sent forth the dove out of the ark; and the dove came in to him in the evening; and, lo, in her mouth was an olive leaf pluckt off: so Noah knew that the waters were abated from off the earth."

"The Thin-Spun Life." Title is from John Milton's elegy *Lycidas:* "Comes the blind *Fury* with th'abhorred shears, / And slits the thin-spun life."

"The Percipient." A "percipient" is one who perceives—i.e., one who sees or knows. The poem gives a twist to Thomas Hardy's "The Impercipient."

"Who Is Wise Among You?" Compare, "Where there is no vision, the people perish" (Proverbs 29:18, KJV).

About the Author

Recipient of the 2014 Writers Exchange Award from Poets & Writers, Harry Moore is the author of three poetry collections: *Bearing the Farm Away* (Kelsay Books, 2018), *Broken and Blended: Love's Alchemy* (Kelsay Books, 2021), and *We the People: Confessions of a Caucasian Southerner* (Broadstone Books, 2024), named 2024 Book of the Year by the Alabama State Poetry Society.

He has also authored four chapbooks: *What He Would Call Them* (Finishing Line Press, 2013), *Time's Fool: Love Poems* (Mule on a Ferris Wheel Press, 2014), *Retreat: A Way Forward* (Finishing Line Press, 2017), and *Beyond Paradise: The Unweeded Garden* (Main Street Rag, 2020).

His poems have appeared in *Sow's Ear Poetry Review, Plainsongs, Xavier Review, Pudding Magazine, Slipstream, Main Street Rag, South Carolina Review, Blue Unicorn, Ponder Review, Anglican Theological Review, Pensive,* and other journals.

Retired after teaching writing and literature for four decades in Alabama community colleges, he lives with his wife, Cassandra, in Decatur, Alabama, and serves on the editorial board of the 7 Points Press.

More info at:
harryvmoore.com